ARIANA GRANDE

by Jim Gigliotti

Consultant: Starshine Roshell
Music and Entertainment Journalist
Santa Barbara, CA

New York, New York

Credits

Cover, © Kristin Callahan/Everett Collection Inc./Alamy; 4, © Splash News/Alamy; 5, © Everett Collection Inc./Alamy; 6, © Foltin/Getty Images; 7, © BSA/ZOJ WENN Photos/Newscom; 8, © Radharc Images/Alamy; 9, © Terry Townsend; 10, Courtesy Seth Poppel/Yearbook Photos; 11, © Greg Campbell/WireImage for Schneider's Bakery/Getty Images; 12, Wikimedia; 13, © Jim Spellman/Getty Images; 14, © Shutterstock; 15, © Splash News/Alamy; 16, © Sbukley/Dreamstime; 17, © Everett Collection/Alamy; 18, © AP Photo/Frank Franklin II; 19, © Starstock/Dreamstime; 20, © Rodruseleg/Dreamstime; 21, © Rex Features via AP Images; 22T, © Starstock/Dreamstime; 22B (phone), © Steveheap/Dreamstime; 22B (Ariana), © Everett Collection, Inc./Alamy; 23, © Everett Collection Inc./Alamy.

Publisher: Kenn Goin
Creative Director: Spencer Brinker
Production and Photo Research: Shoreline Publishing Group LLC

Library of Congress Cataloging-in-Publication Data

Names: Gigliotti, Jim, author.
Title: Ariana Grande / by Jim Gigliotti.
Description: New York, New York : Bearport Publishing, [2018] | Series:
    Amazing Americans: pop music stars | Includes bibliographical references
    and index.
Identifiers: LCCN 2017045545 (print) | LCCN 2017045587 (ebook) |
ISBN 9781684025169 (ebook) | ISBN 9781684024582 (library)
Subjects: LCSH: Grande, Ariana—Juvenile literature. | Singers—United
    States—Biography—Juvenile literature. | Actresses—United
    States—Biography—Juvenile literature.
Classification: LCC ML3930.G724 (ebook) | LCC ML3930.G724 G54 2018 (print) |
    DDC 782.42164092 [B] —dc23
LC record available at https://lccn.loc.gov/2017045545

For more information, write to Bearport Publishing Company, Inc., 45 West 21st Street, Suite 3B, New York, New York 10010. Printed in the United States of America.

10 9 8 7 6 5 4 3 2 1

CONTENTS

Pop Superstar!

Ariana Grande came onstage, and the crowd went wild. It was 2014, and the pop music superstar was performing in New York. For 90 minutes, she sang and danced. The **arena** rocked with energy and excitement—just like Ariana's music!

Ariana poses for a selfie with a fan.

Ariana's music videos have been viewed online more than 8 billion times.

5

Born in the U.S.A.

Ariana Grande-Butera was born on June 26, 1993, in Boca Raton, Florida. From an early age, Ariana wanted a **career** in music. She started dreaming about it when she was just three years old!

Ariana with her brother, Frankie

Ariana shopping with her mom, Joan

Ariana's name was inspired by Princess Oriana in the movie *Felix the Cat*.

Discovered

Ariana and her family took a cruise when she was eight. She sang a song on the ship just for fun. Gloria Estefan, a famous singer, was also on the cruise. When she heard Ariana sing, she was amazed! She encouraged Ariana to follow her dream.

Singer Gloria Estefan

Ariana as Cinderella

In grade school, Ariana performed with the Fort Lauderdale Children's Theater.

9

Doing Good

Ariana learned she could have fun singing while helping others. In 2003, she formed a singing group called Kids Who Care. It raised money for **charities** near her South Florida home.

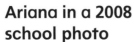

In 2007, Kids Who Care helped raise more than $500,000 for charities.

Ariana in a 2008 school photo

10

In 2011, Ariana visited kids at St. Jude Children's Research Hospital in Memphis, Tennessee.

11

Stage and Screen

Ariana became a **professional** singer and actress in 2008. She sang in a musical called *13*. She won a national theater award for her performance. Then in 2009, she became a TV actress. She played Cat Valentine on *Victorious* and *Sam & Cat*.

In 2012, *Victorious* won the Nickelodeon Kids' Choice Award.

Ariana (far right) with the cast of *Victorious*

Ariana at a gathering for the musical *13*

Living the Dream

Music was always Ariana's biggest dream. "If you want something, you really have to go for it," she has said. That is just what she did! In 2013, she finished an album called *Yours Truly*. In its first week, it was the number one selling album in the United States.

In 2013, Ariana was an opening singer on Justin Bieber's *Believe* Tour.

Ariana signs a CD of *Yours Truly* for New York fans in 2014.

Music Mix

Ariana's music **genre** is pop, with some rhythm and blues (R&B) mixed in. Her **idols** are R&B stars such as Whitney Houston and Mariah Carey. Ariana's music also includes funk, hip-hop, and more. Her singing appeals to many different music fans.

Superstar singer Mariah Carey

Ariana has more than 14 million Instagram followers!

17

Artist of the Year

In 2014, Ariana released her second album called *My Everything*. It also became the number-one album in the United States. Two years later, she released *Dangerous Woman*. It was another hit album. In 2016, she was named Artist of the Year by the American Music Awards (AMA)!

Ariana performed during halftime at the NBA All-Star Game in 2015.

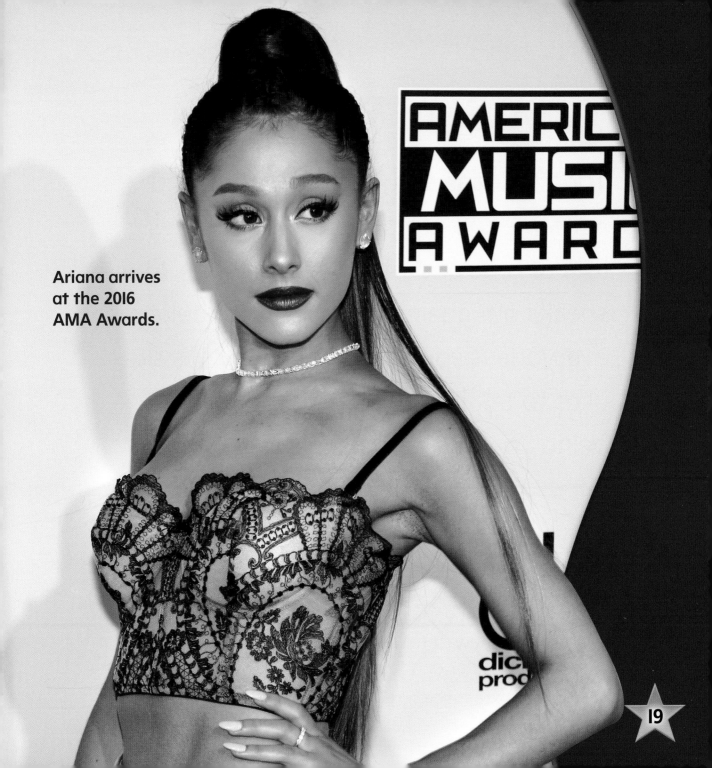

Ariana arrives at the 2016 AMA Awards.

AMERIC
MUSI
AWARD

dic
prod

A Star Who Cares

Today, Ariana still uses her music and her fame to help people. She donates lots of time and money to charities. She speaks out against bullying. She believes everyone is special in some way. As she likes to tell her fans, "Be happy with being you!"

In May 2017, a bomb exploded during Ariana's concert in Manchester, England. Many people were hurt. Some were killed. Less than two weeks later, Ariana put on a special show. It raised $13 million to help victims and their families.

Ariana sings in Manchester to help victims of the attack.

21

Timeline

Here are some key dates in Ariana Grande's life.

1990   2000   2010   2020

June 26, 1993
Ariana Grande-Butera is born in Boca Raton, Florida.

2003
Forms singing group called Kids Who Care

2008
Performs in the musical *13*

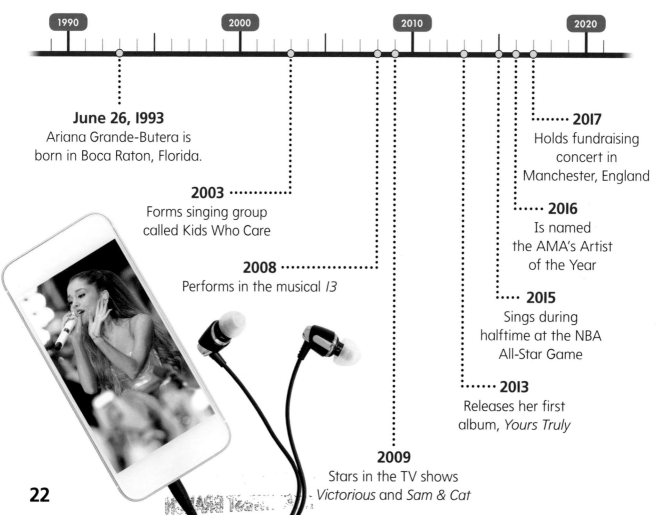

2009
Stars in the TV shows *Victorious* and *Sam & Cat*

2013
Releases her first album, *Yours Truly*

2015
Sings during halftime at the NBA All-Star Game

2016
Is named the AMA's Artist of the Year

2017
Holds fundraising concert in Manchester, England

Glossary

arena (uh-REE-nuh) an indoor place where sporting events or concerts are held

career (ka-REER) a job or field of work that is done for a long time

charities (CHA-ruh-tees) organizations that raise money to help people in need

genre (ZHAN-ruh) a kind of music, art, or literature

idols (EYE-dulls) admired people

professional (proh-FESH-uh-null) a person who gets paid for what he or she does

Index

Read More

Klein, Emily. *Ariana Grande: Truly Yours.* New York: Scholastic (2015).

Morreale, Marie. *Ariana Grande (Real Bios).* New York: Children's Press (2014).

Learn More Online

To learn more about Ariana Grande, visit
www.bearportpublishing.com/AmazingAmericans

About the Author

Jim Gigliotti is a former editor at the National Football League. He now writes books on a variety of topics for young readers.